39 progressive solos for Classical guitar
With Tablature
Book II

Arranged by Ben Bolt

• Classical Guitar Tablature Explanation/Notation Legend •

TABLATURE: A six-line staff that graphically represents the guitar fingerboard, with the top line indicating the highest-sounding string (high E). By placing a number on the appropriate line, the string and fret of any note can be indicated. The number 0 represents an open string.

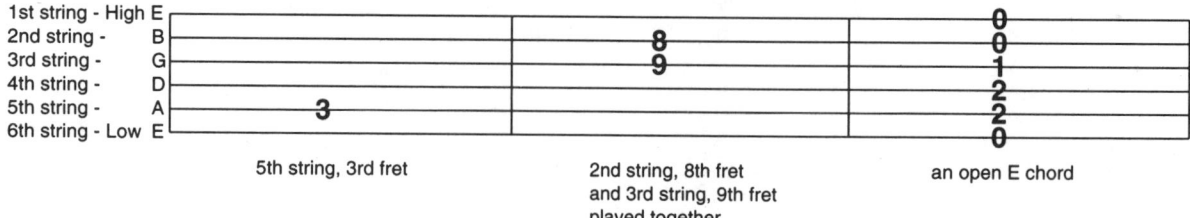

Definitions for Special Classical Guitar Notation

Stem Direction and Right-Hand Fingering: In music of two or more parts, notes with downward stems are played by the thumb; notes with upward stems are played by the fingers; a note with a double stem (up and down) is played by the thumb. The letters *p*, *i*, *m* and *a* are used to specify which right-hand fingers are to play the indicated notes (*p* = thumb; *i* = index; *m* = middle; *a* = ring).

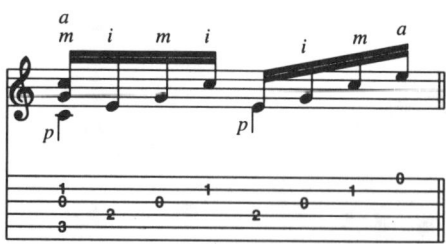

Barre: The letter C and accompanying Roman numeral indicate which fret is to be barred by the left hand. A dotted line indicates how long the barre is to be held.

Fractional Barre: The fraction preceding the letter C indicates how many strings the left hand covers when barring. For example, 2/3C means to barre the top four strings, 1/2C the top three strings, etc.

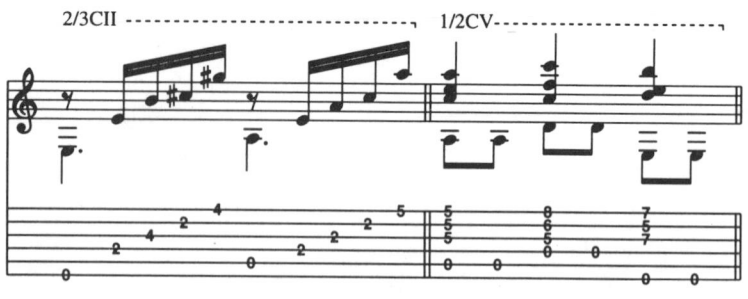

String Numbers and Left-Hand Fingering:
Numbers inside circles indicate on which string a note is to be played, and uncircled numbers indicate which left-hand fingers to use (1 = index; 2 = middle; 3 = ring; 4 = little).

Slurs: An ascending slur is executed by a hammer-on. A descending slur is executed by a pull-off. A straight line connecting two slurred notes indicates a slide.

Arpeggios: A vertical wavy line indicates the notes are to be played quickly by rolling them from bottom to top (no arrowhead present) or top to bottom (arrowhead pointing down).

Harmonic: A harmonic is produced by the left hand lightly touching the string over the node point while simultaneously plucking with the right hand.

Artificial Harmonic: The note is fretted normally and a harmonic is produced by lightly touching the node point with the right-hand index finger while simultaneously plucking with the right-hand middle or ring finger.

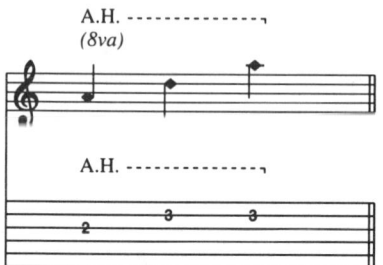

Contents Book I

	Page	Track
1 Study 1 (Aguado)	3	1
2 Study 2 (Carcassi)	4	2
3 Study 3 (Carcassi)	4	2
4 Study 4 (Carcassi)	6	3
5 Study 5 (Carcassi)	6	3
6 Study 6 (Giuliani)	7	4
7 Study 7 (Carcassi)	8	5
8 Study 8 (Carcassi)	11	6
9 Study 9 (Giuliani)	12	6
10 Study 10 (Giuliani)	13	7
11 Study 11 (Aguado)	14	8
12 Study 12 (Giuliani)	15	9
13 Joyful, Joyful We Adore Thee (Beethoven)	17	10
14 Rondo (Carcassi)	18	11
15 Allegretto (Carulli)	20	12
16 Waltz (Carcassi)	23	13
17 Maestoso (Giuliani)	25	14
18 Scarborough Fair (Anonymous)	26	15
19 Vivace (Giuliani)	28	16
20 Estudio (Carulli)	30	17
21 Grazioso (Giuliani)	33	18
22 Allegro (Giuliani)	34	19
23 Etude (Carcassi)	36	20
24 Lagrima (Tarrega)	40	21
25 Moderato (Giuliani)	41	22
26 Study In A (Carcassi)	44	23
27 Bouree (J.S. Bach)	46	24

Contents Book II

	Page	Track
1 Study In C (Sor)	4	1
2 Study In B Minor (Sor)	6	2
3 Song Of The Emperor (de Narváez)	9	3
4 Romance (Anonymous)	13	4
5 Six Pavans (Milan)	16	5
6 Study In D (Sor)	29	6
7 Sarabande (J.S. Bach)	32	7
8 Tarleton's Resurrection (Dowland)	34	8
9 Guárdame Las Vacas (de Narváez)	35	9
10 Baxa De Contrapunto (de Narváez)	37	10
11 Allemande (J.S. Bach)	40	11
12 Canarios (Sanz)	42	12

Each book is available with CD or with cassette. Numbers in boxes refer to CD and cassette tracks.

1

STUDY IN C

Arr. Ben Bolt

Fernando Sor

Allegretto

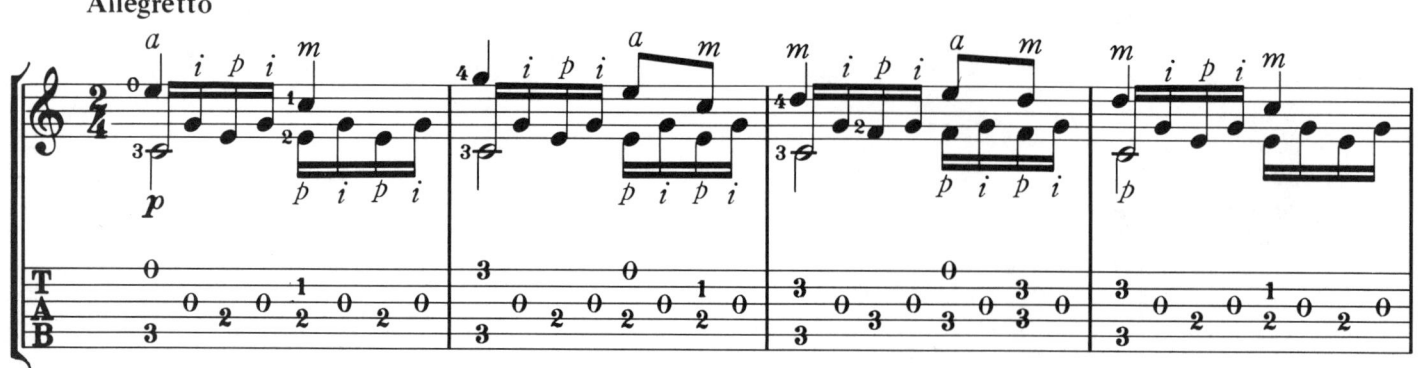

*Numbers in boxes refer to CD and cassette tracks.

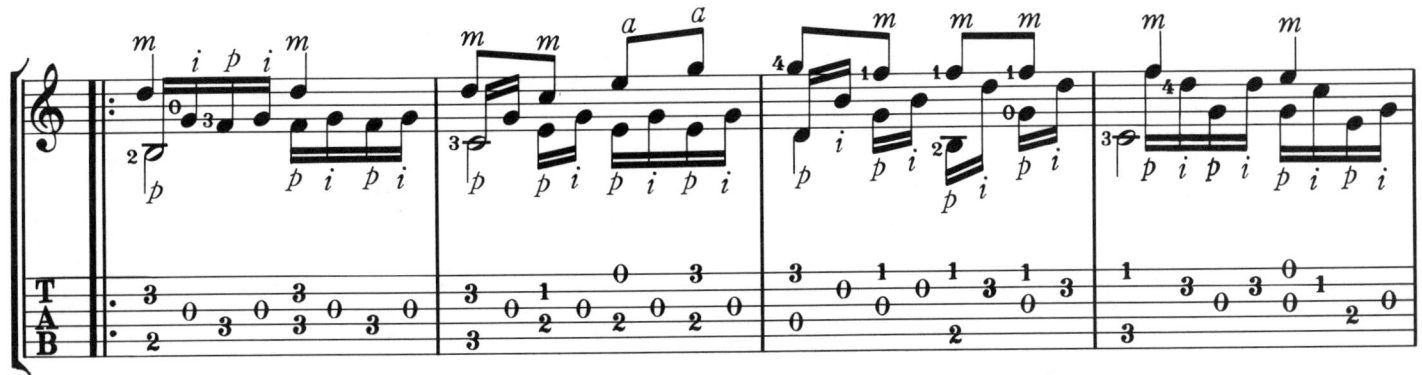

2
STUDY IN B MINOR

Arr. Ben Bolt

Fernando Sor

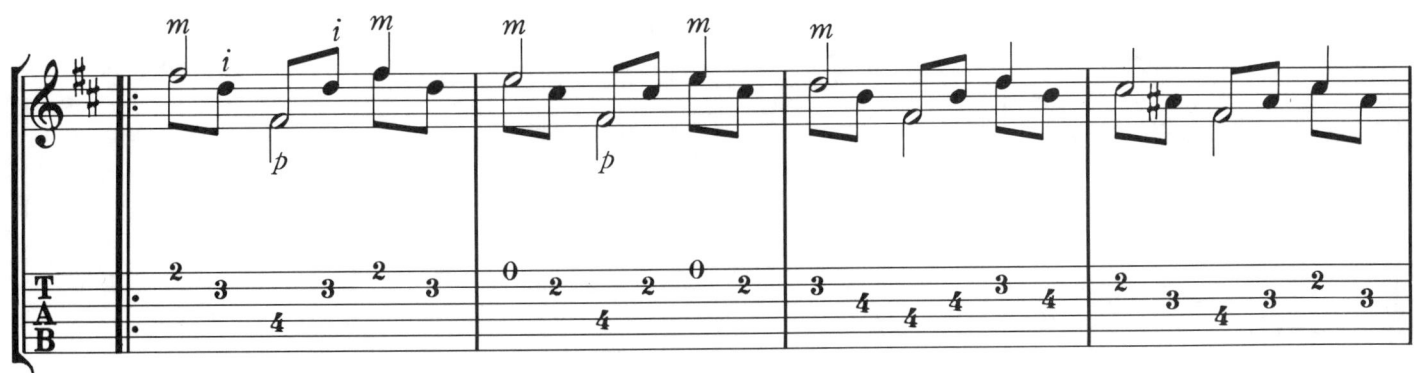
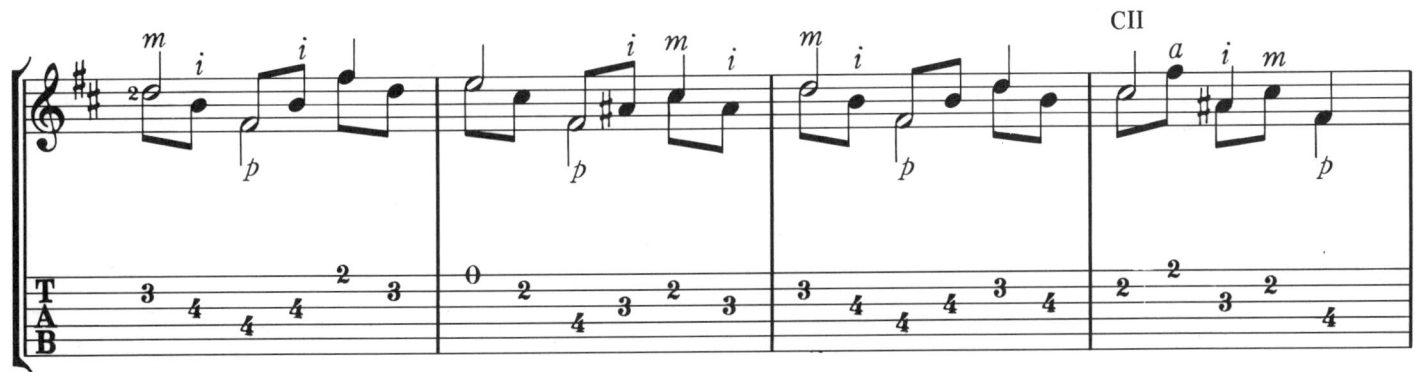

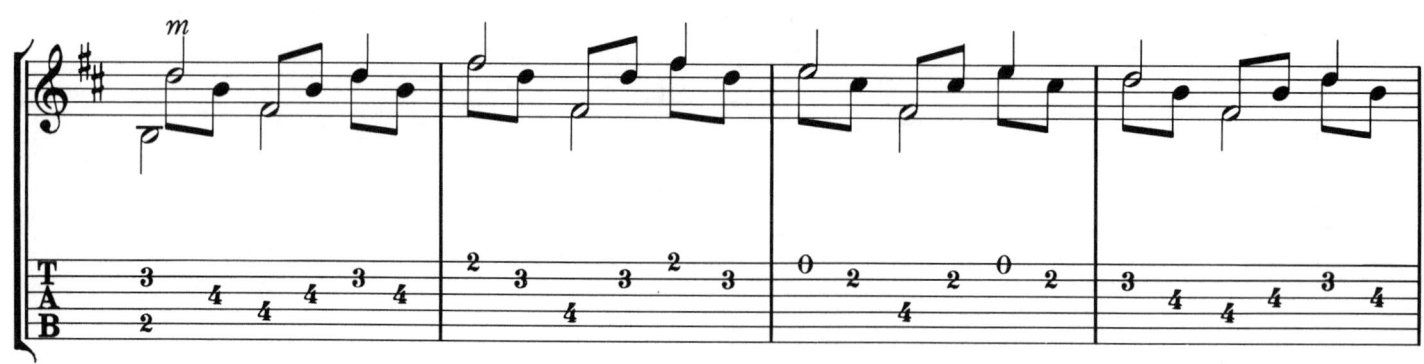

3

SONG OF THE EMPEROR

Arr. Ben Bolt

Luys de Narváez

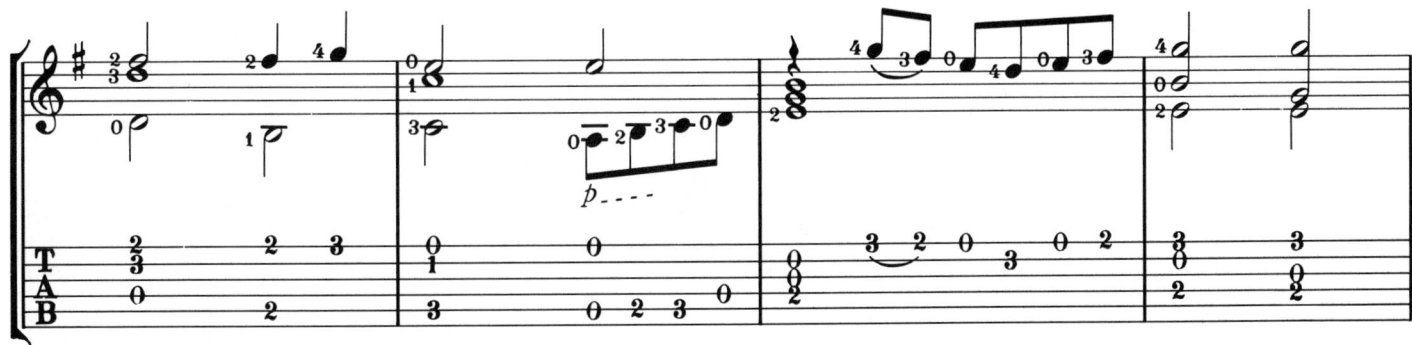
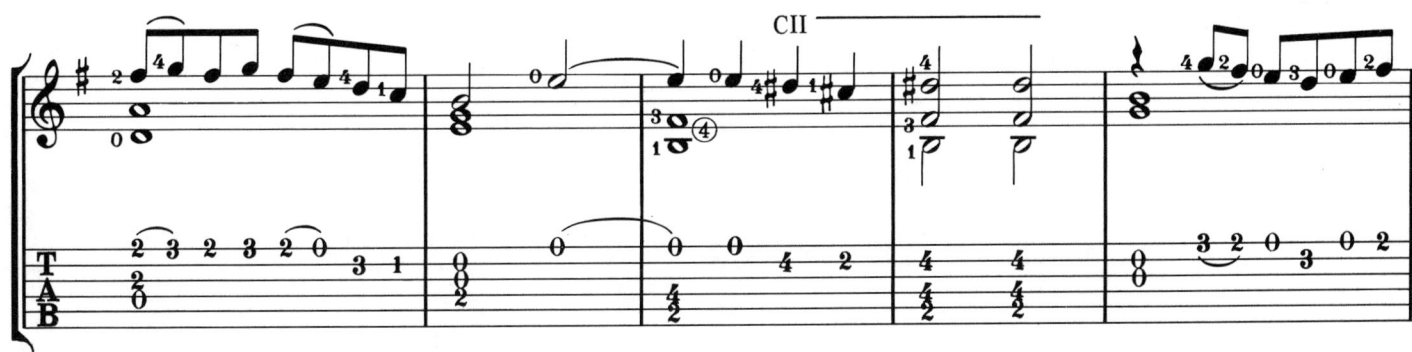

This Arrangement © 1991 Cherry Lane Music Company, Inc.
International Copyright Secured All Rights Reserved

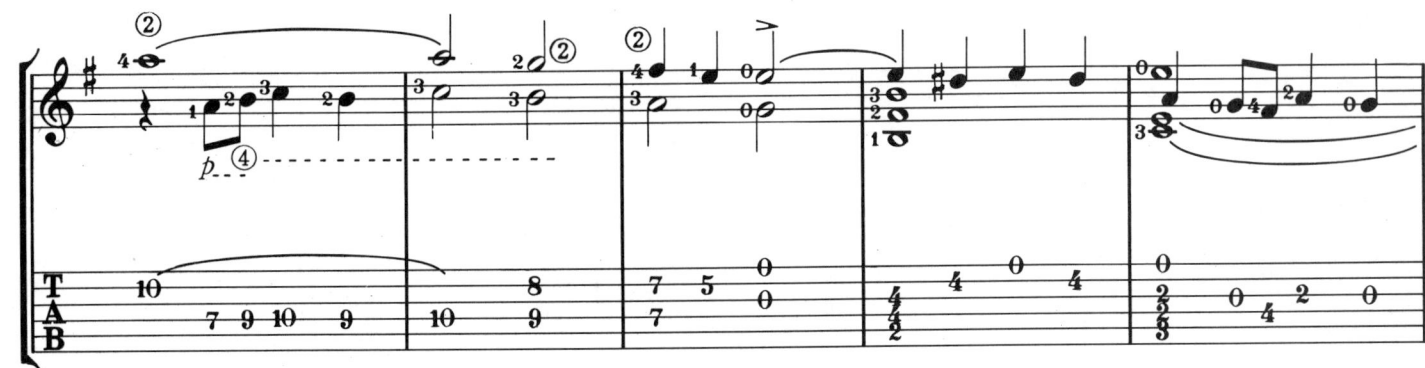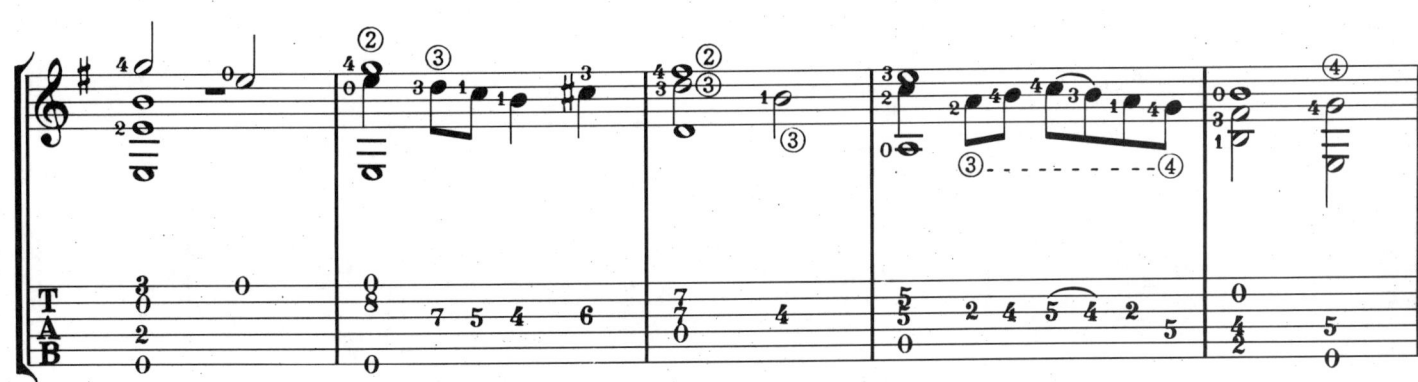

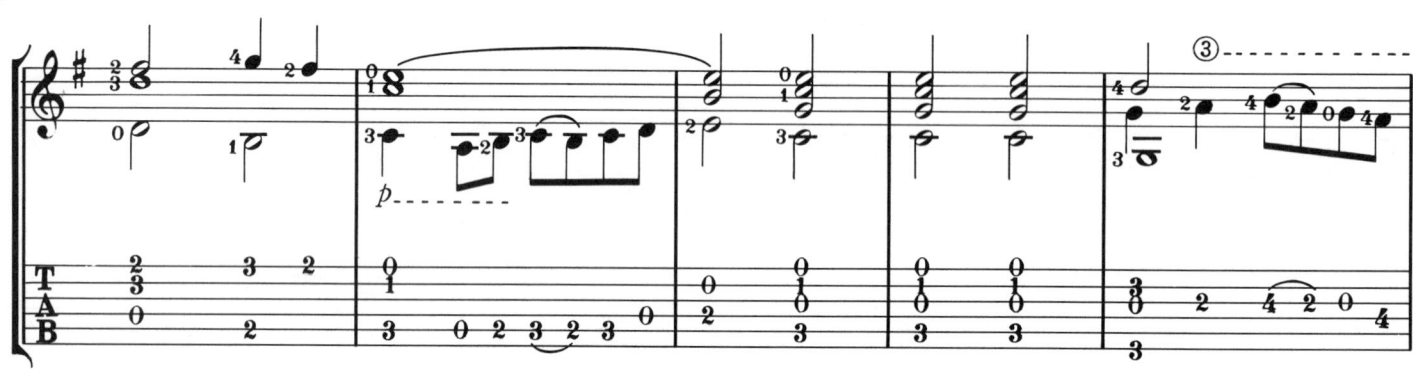
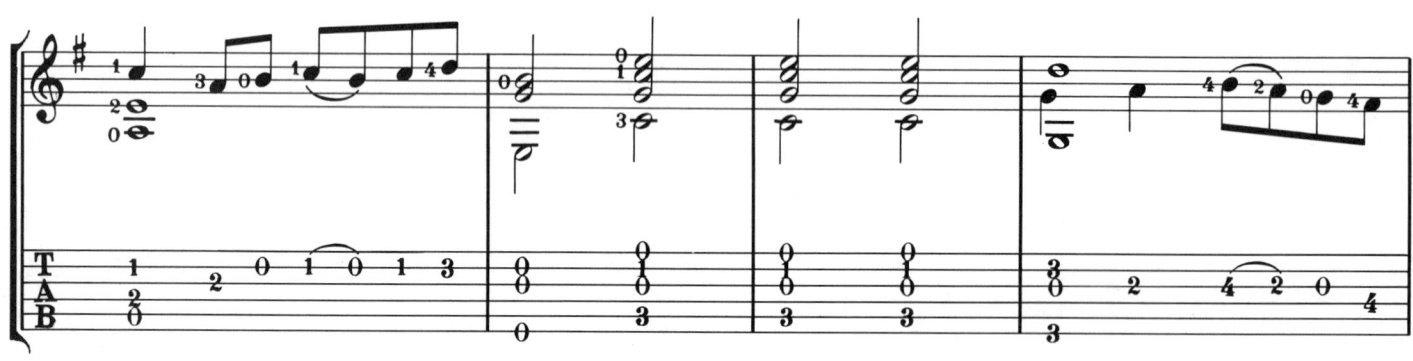
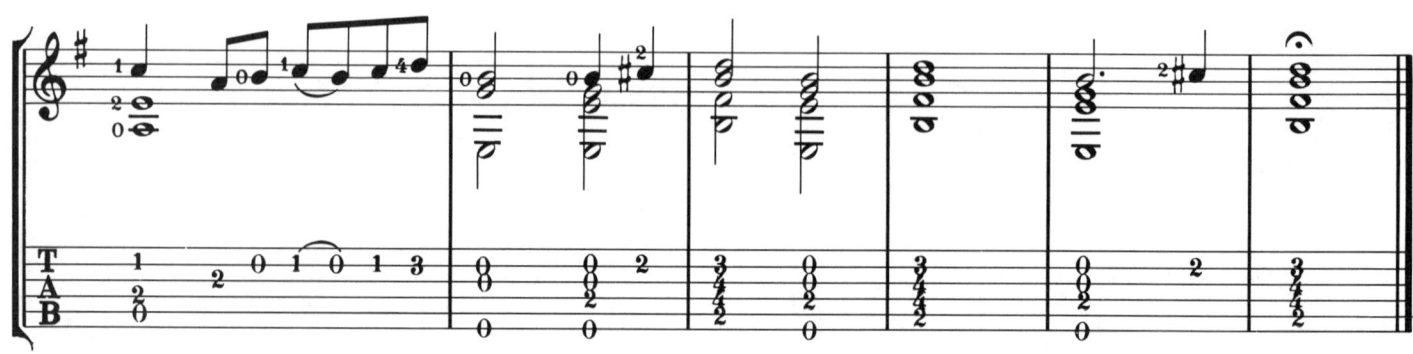

ROMANCE

Arr. Ben Bolt

Anonymous

This Arrangement © 1991 Cherry Lane Music Company, Inc.
International Copyright Secured All Rights Reserved

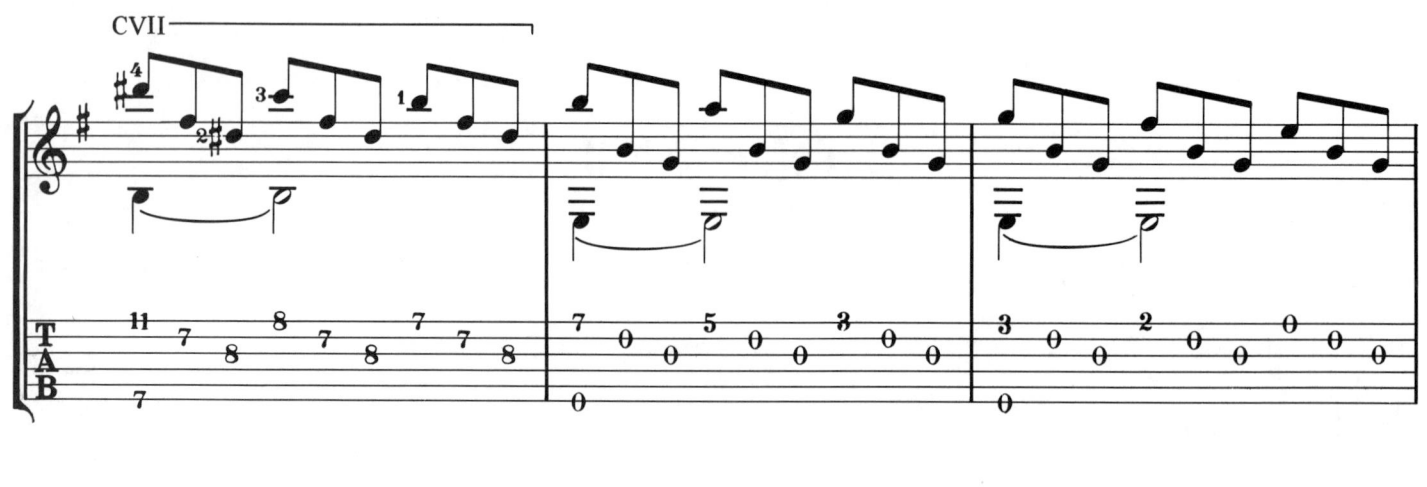
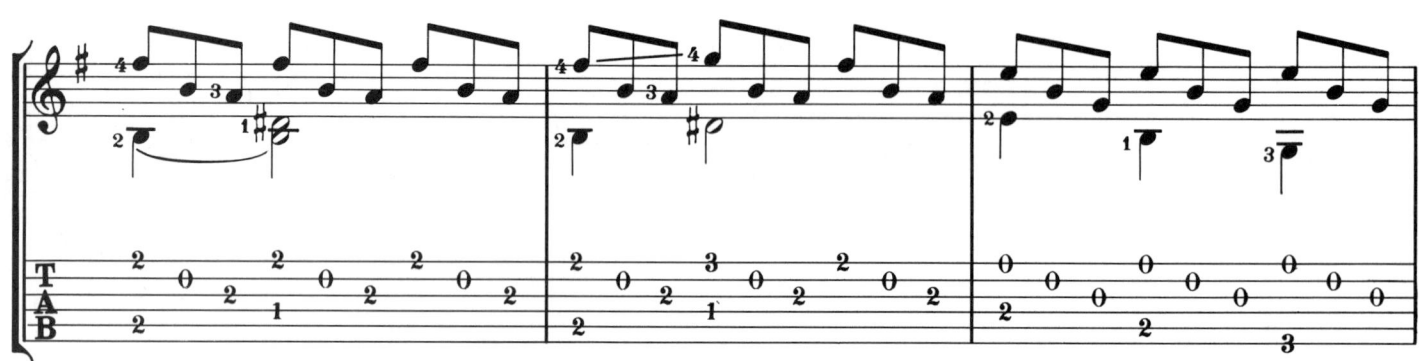

Fine
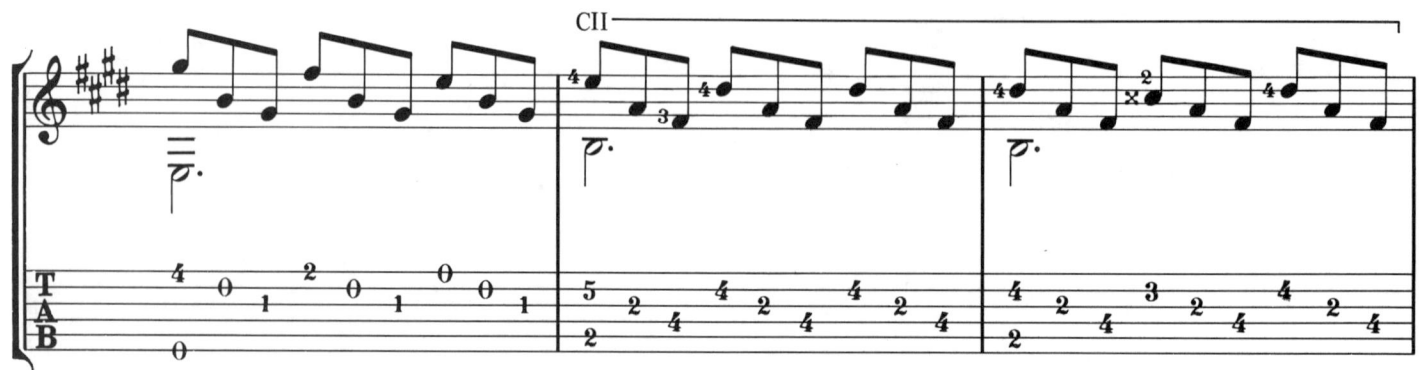

D.C. al Fine

5

SIX PAVANS

Arr. Ben Bolt

Luis Milan

1

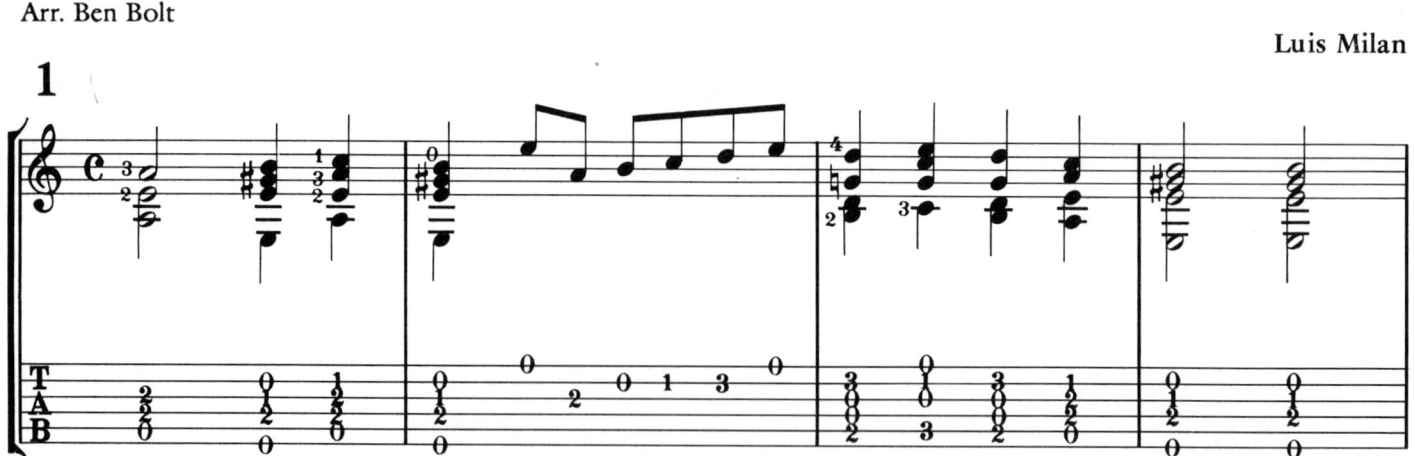

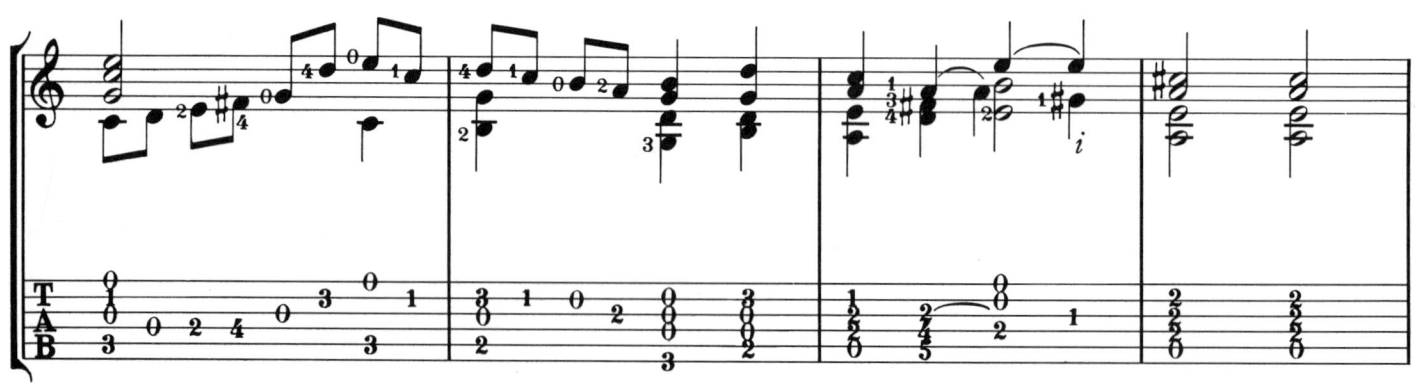

This Arrangement © 1991 Cherry Lane Music Company, Inc.
International Copyright Secured All Rights Reserved

2

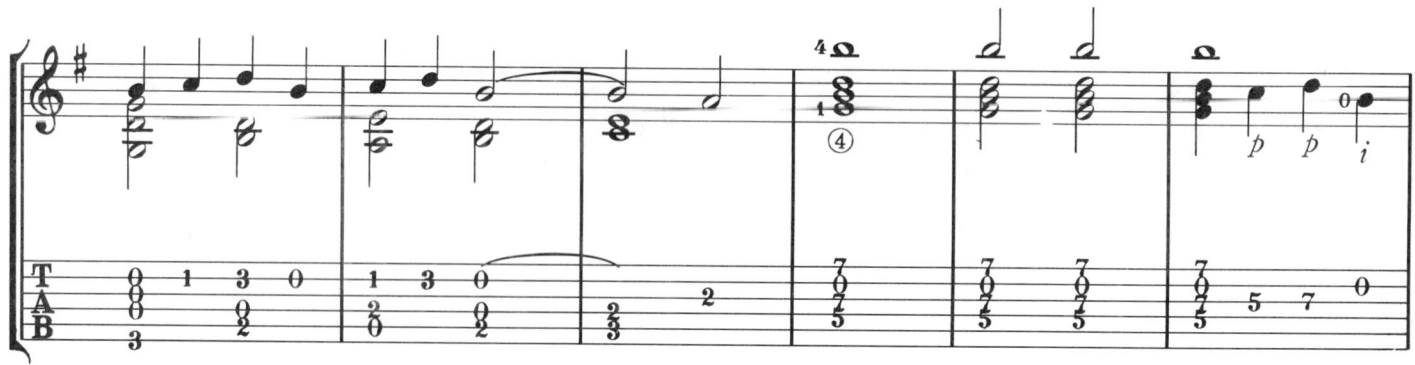
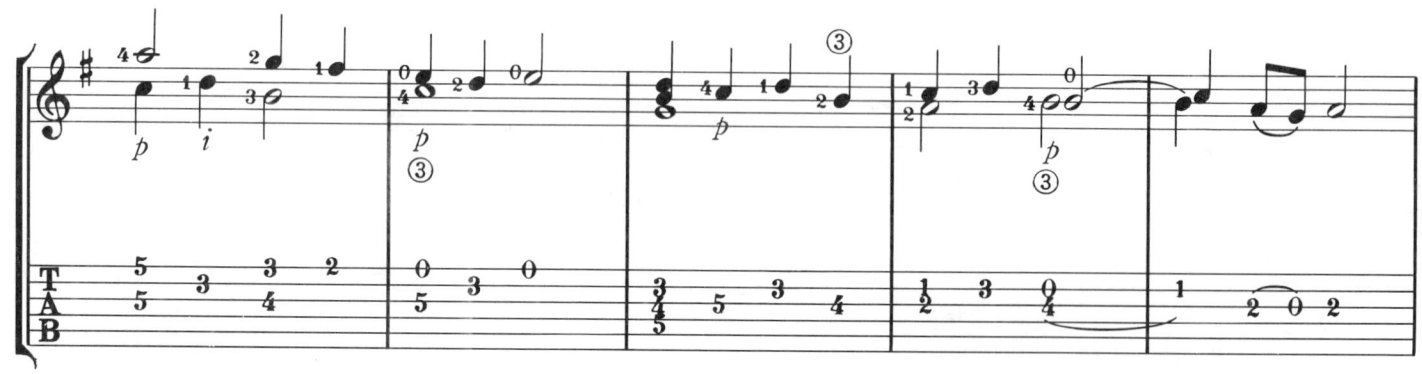
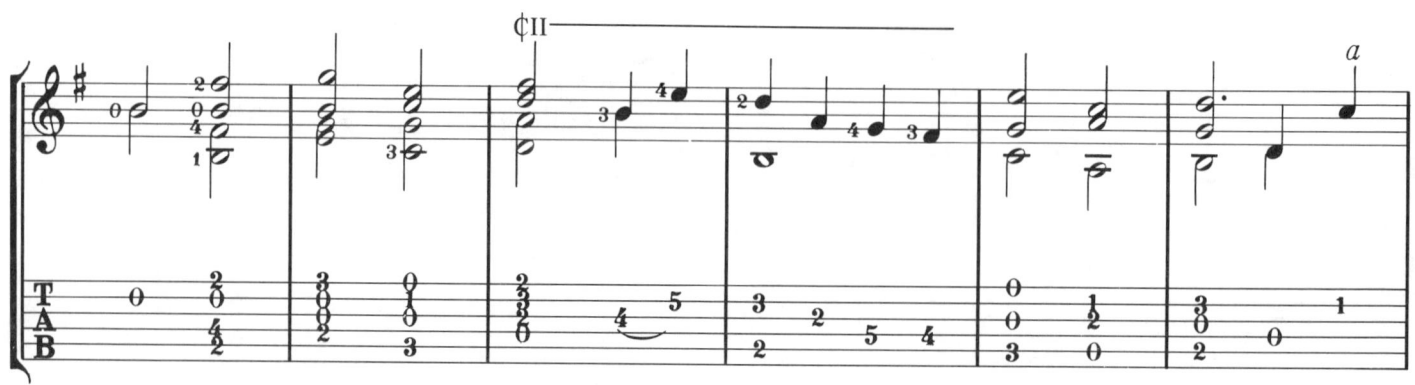

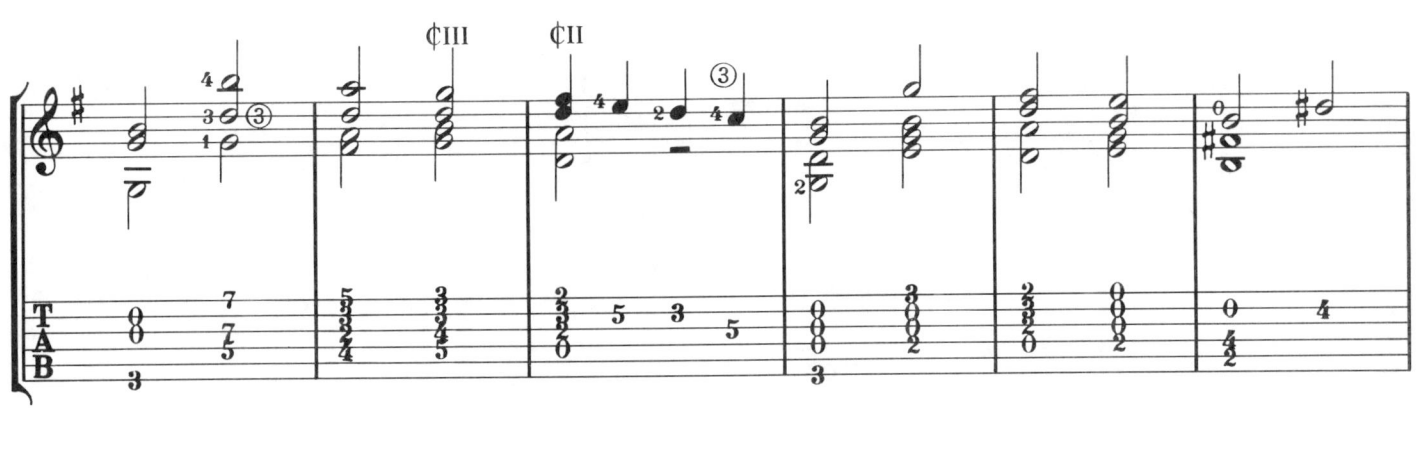

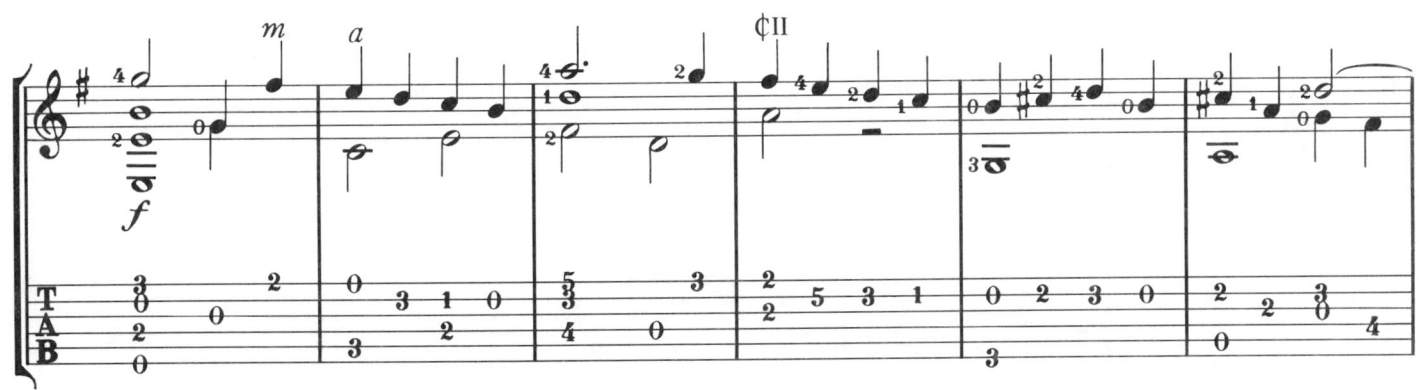
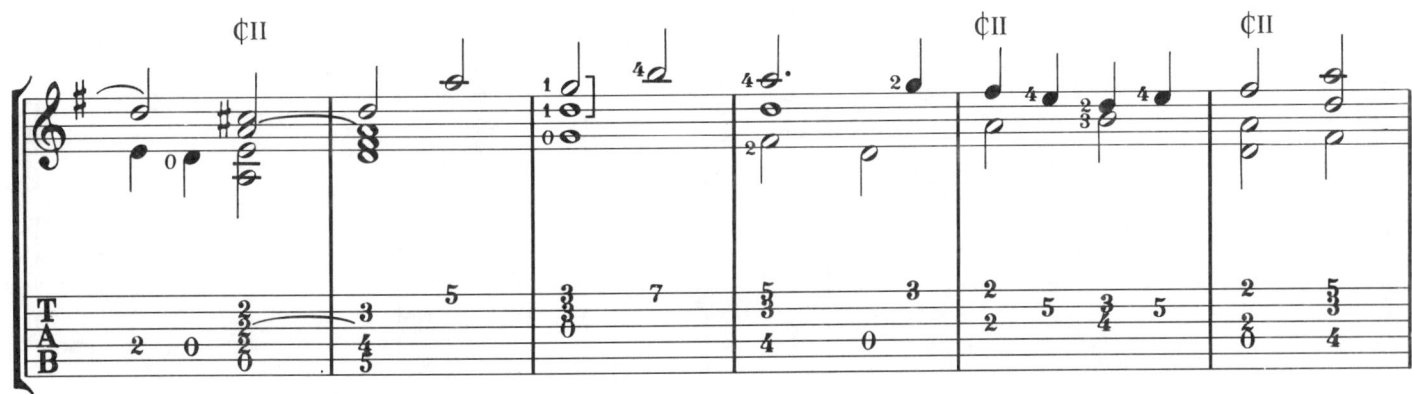

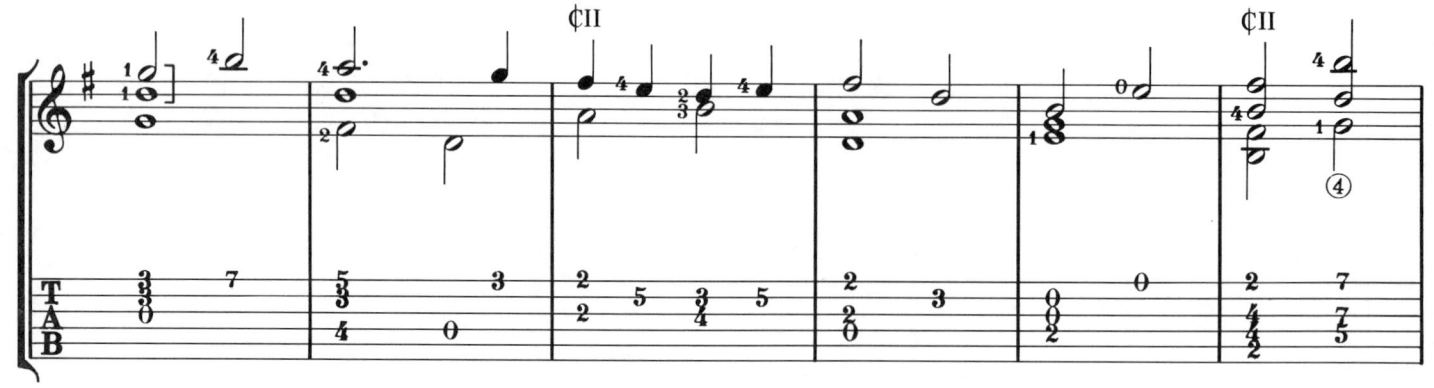
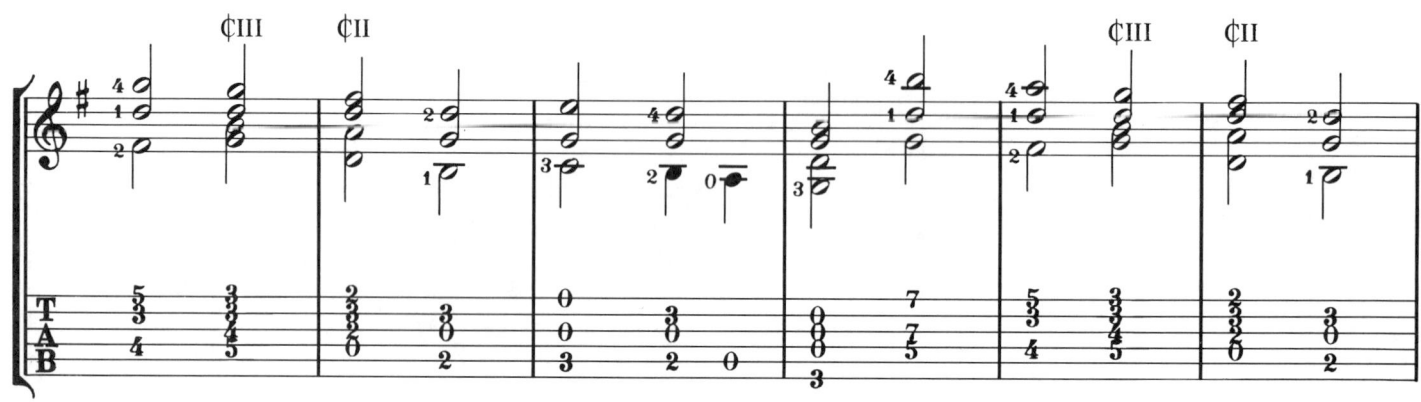

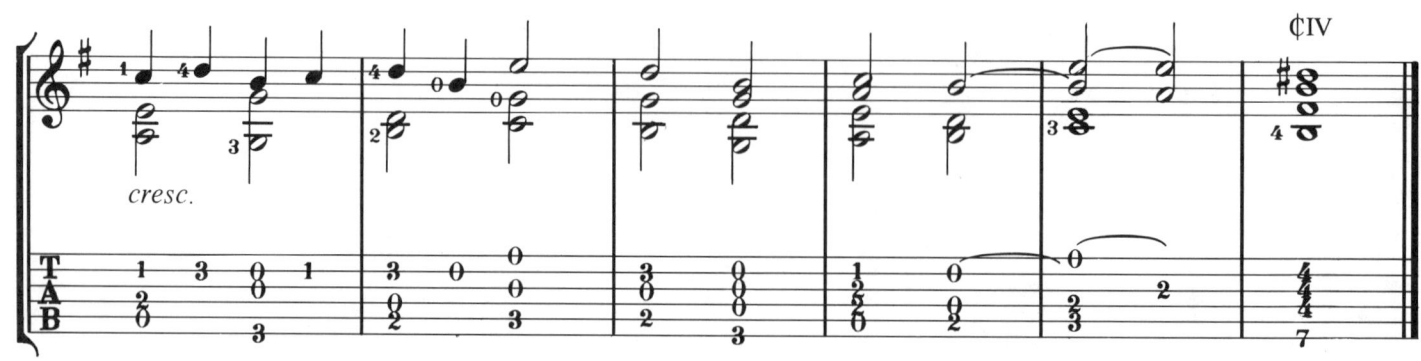

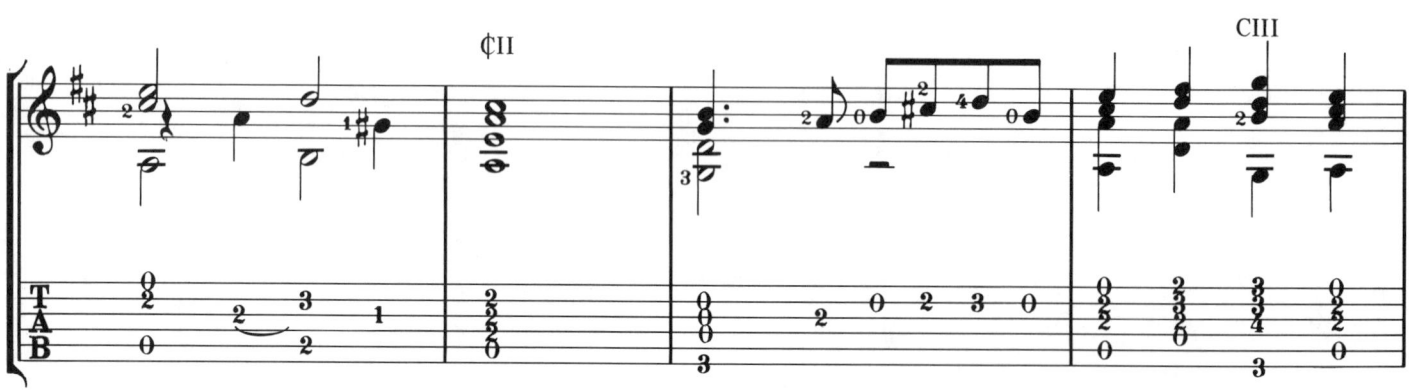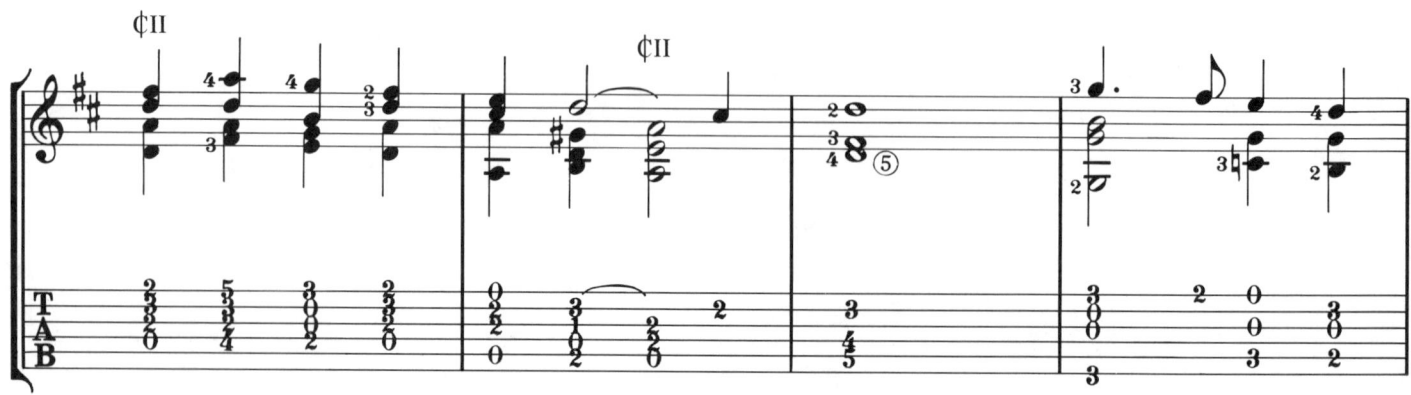

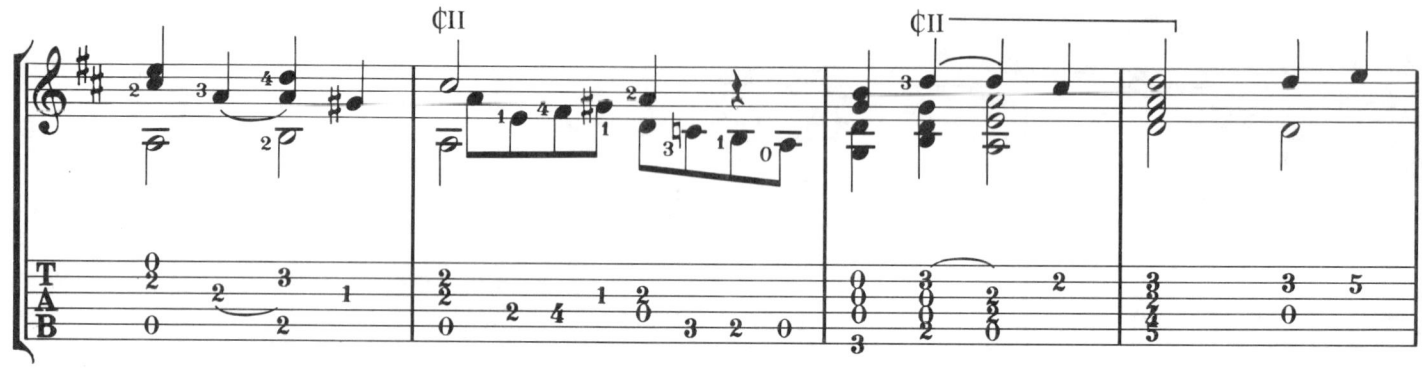

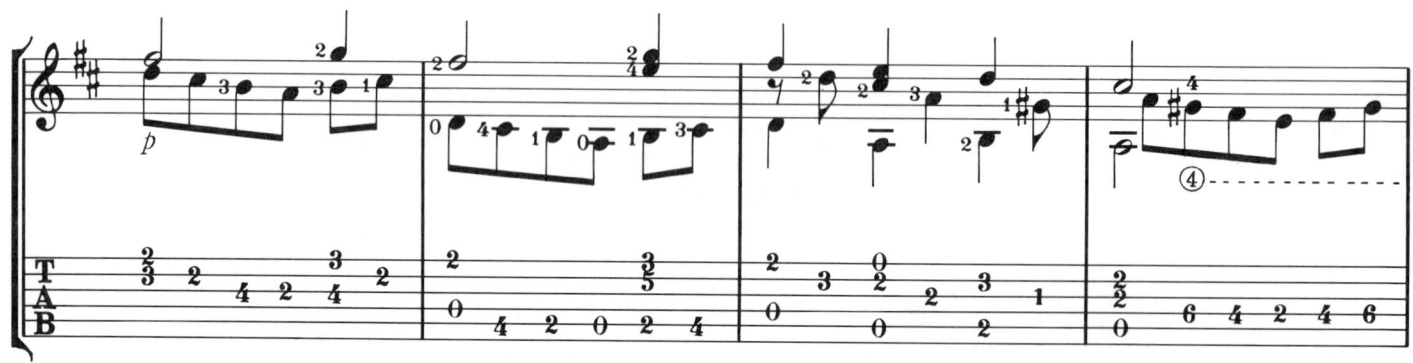
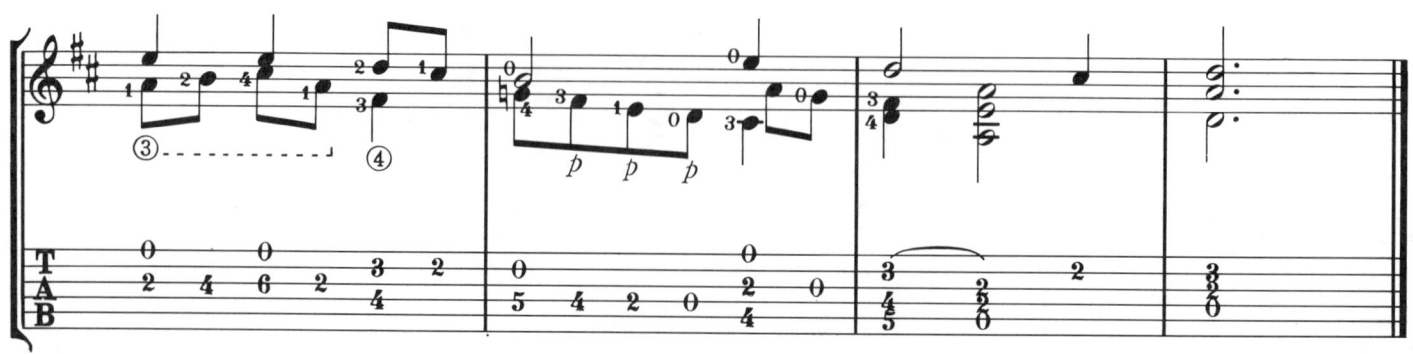

6
STUDY IN D

Arr. Ben Bolt (1978)
Fernando Sor

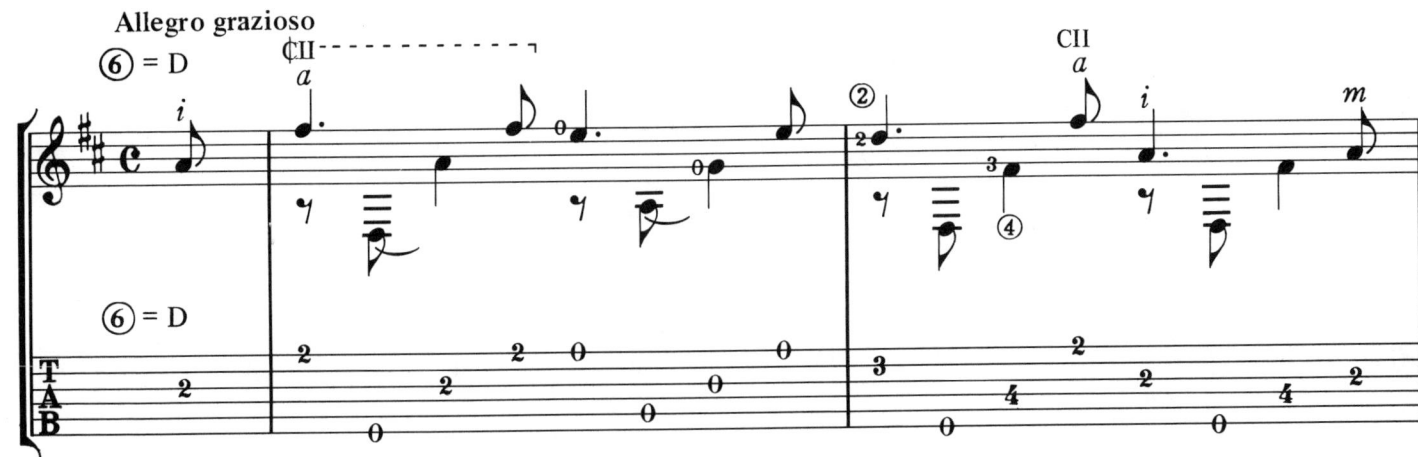

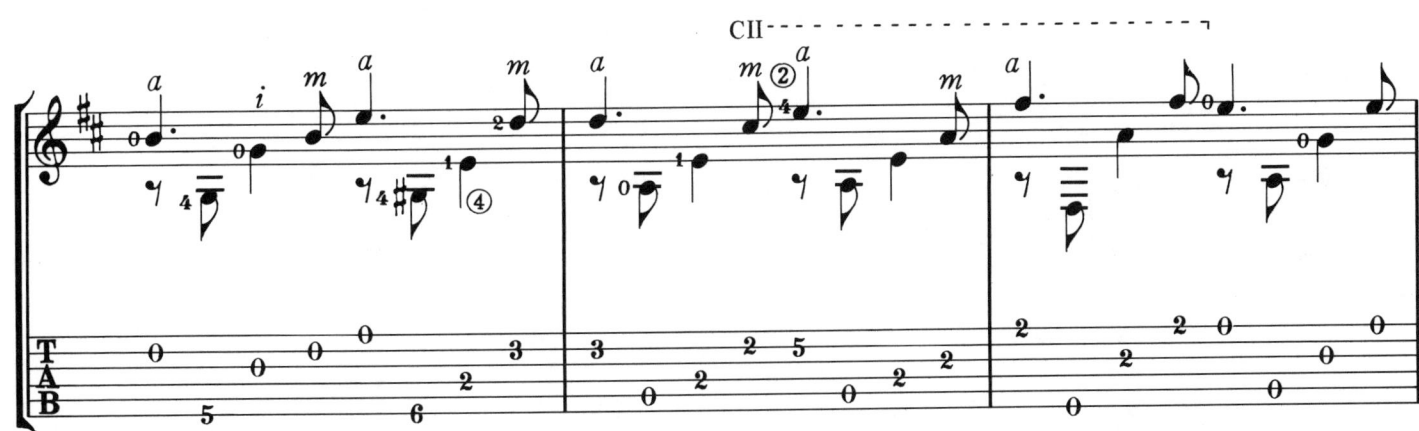

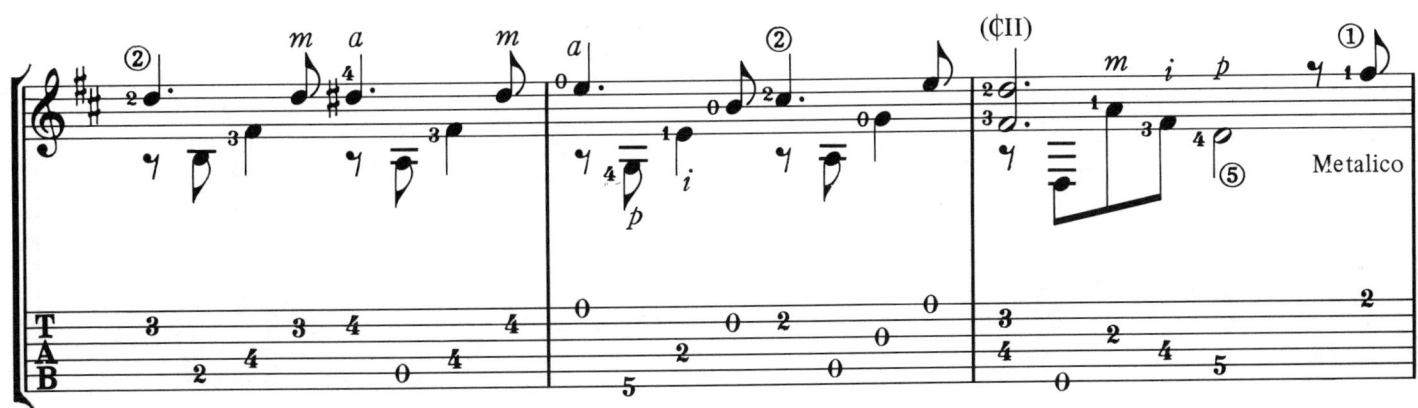

This Arrangement © 1991 Cherry Lane Music Company, Inc.
International Copyright Secured All Rights Reserved

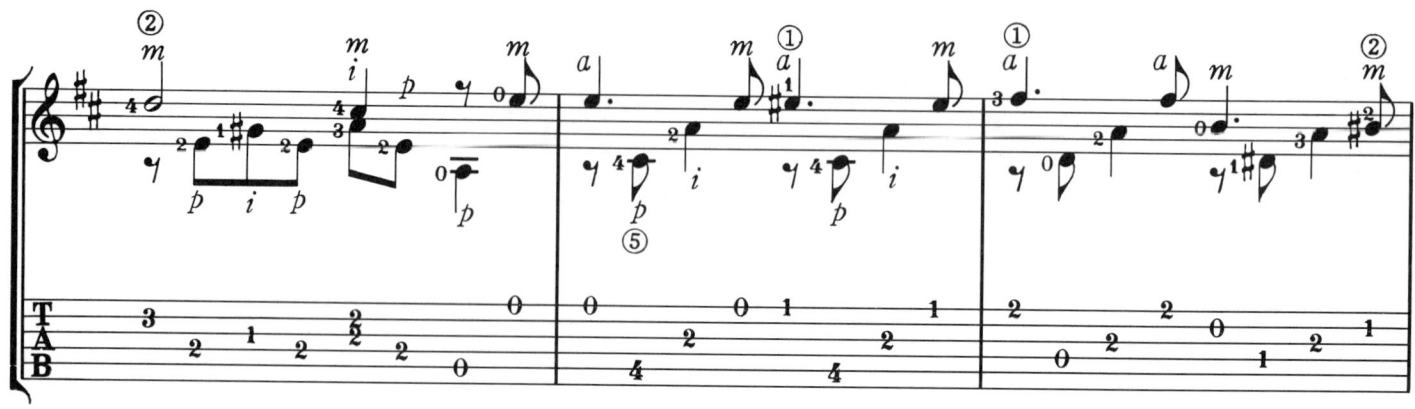
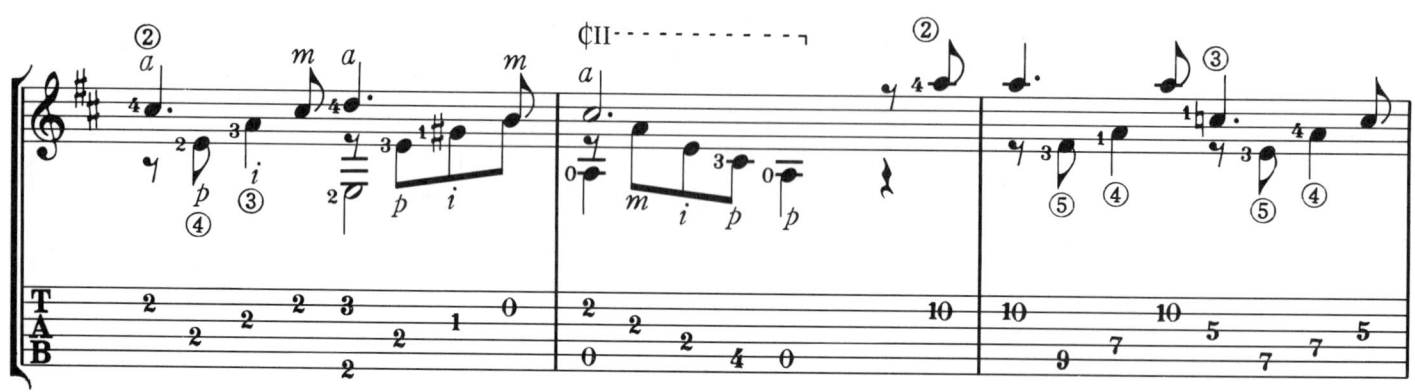
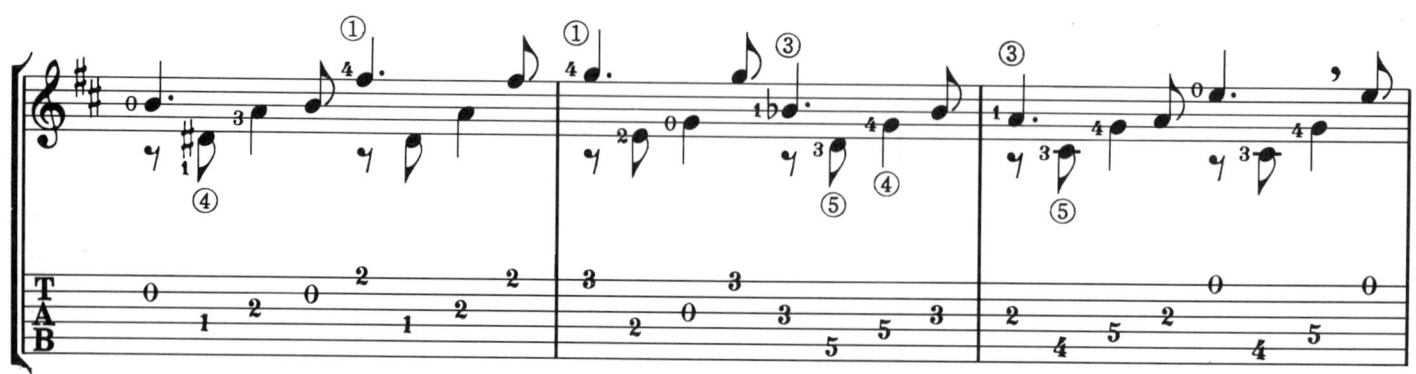

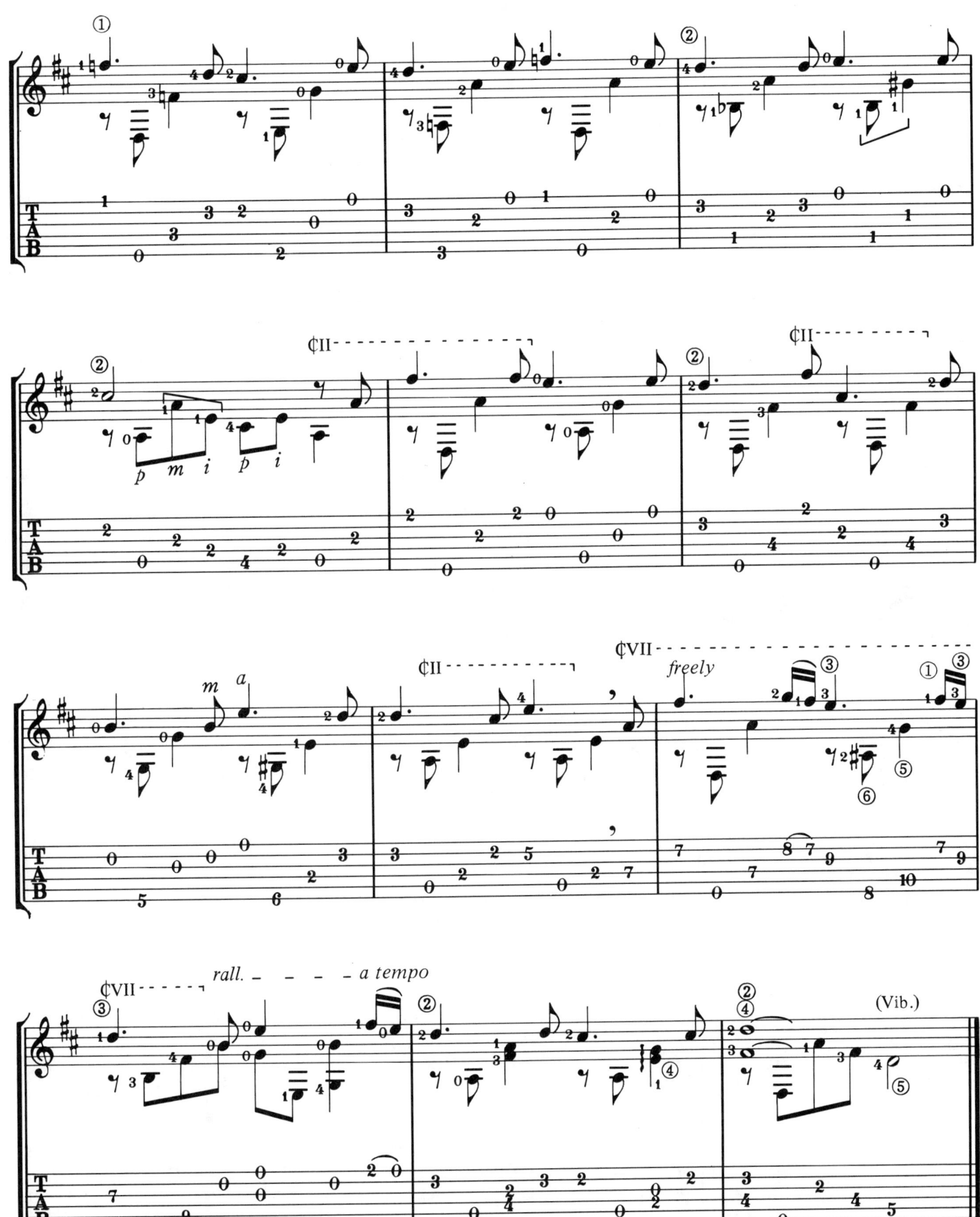

7

SARABANDE
from Partita No.1 in B minor for Violin solo

Arr. Ben Bolt

J. S. BACH

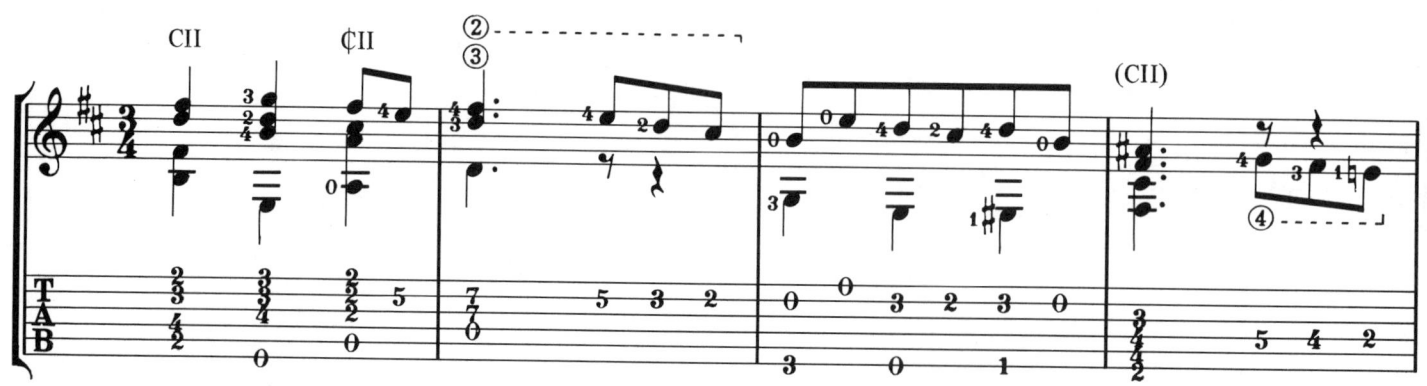

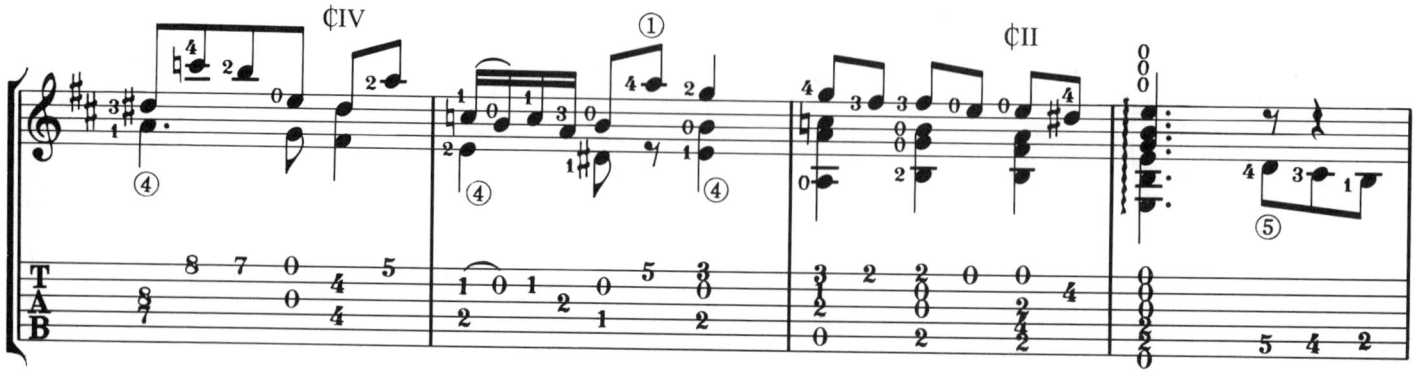

This Arrangement © 1991 Cherry Lane Music Company, Inc.
International Copyright Secured All Rights Reserved

8

TARLETON'S RESURRECTION

Arr. Ben Bolt

John Dowland

9
GUÁRDAME LAS VACAS

Arr. Ben Bolt

Luys de Narváez

This Arrangement © 1991 Cherry Lane Music Company, Inc.
International Copyright Secured All Rights Reserved

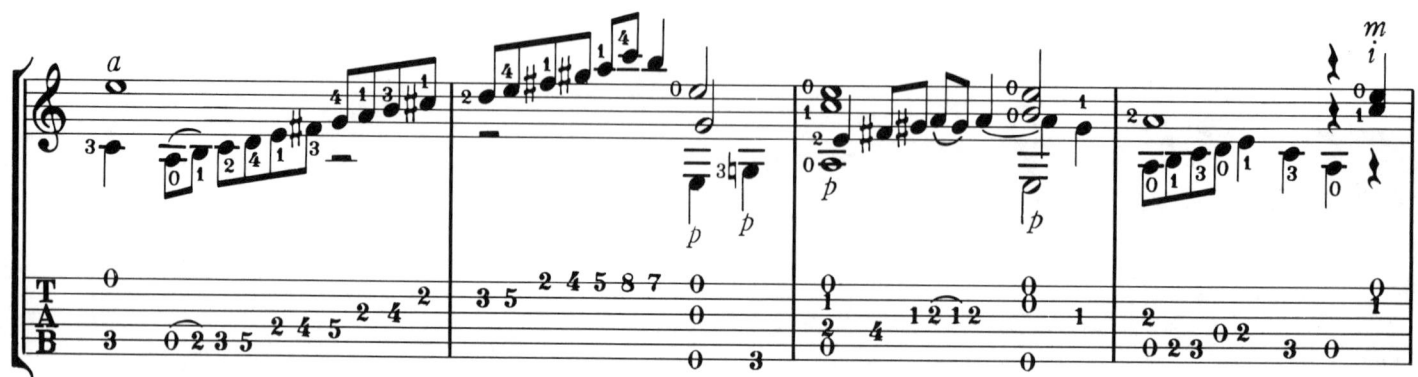

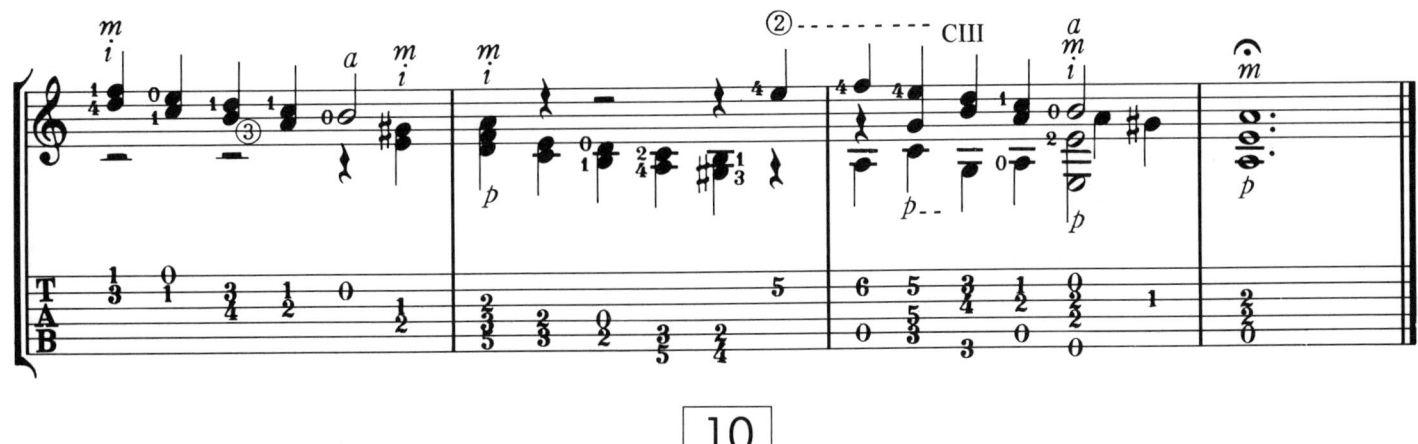

10

BAXA DE CONTRAPUNTO

Arr. Ben Bolt

Luys de Narváez

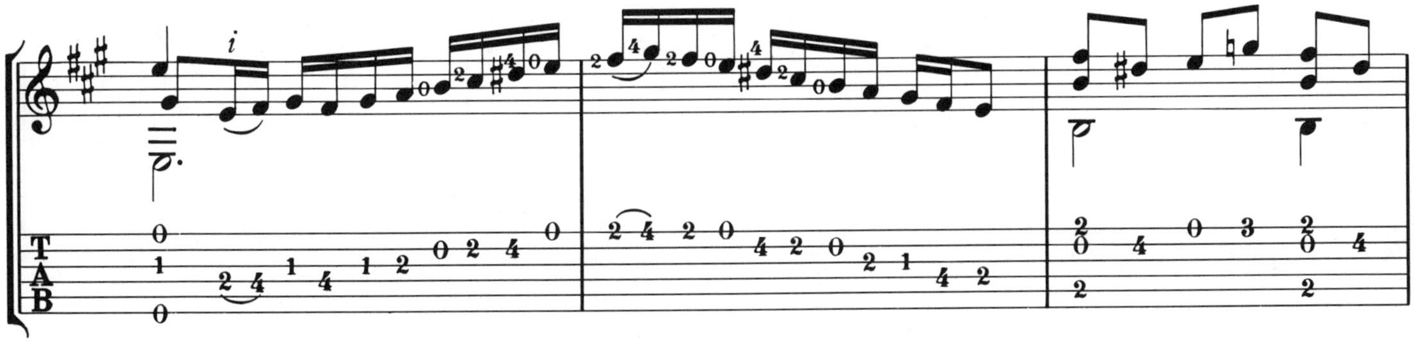

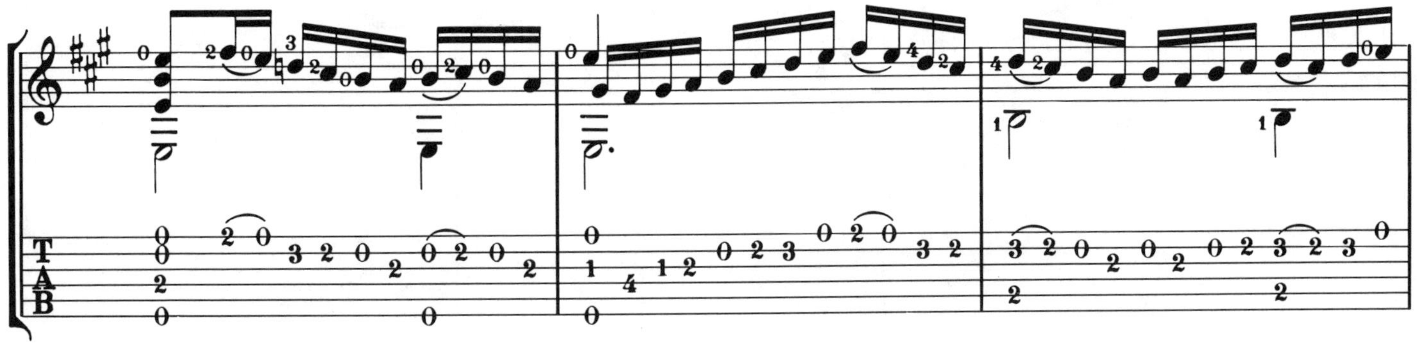

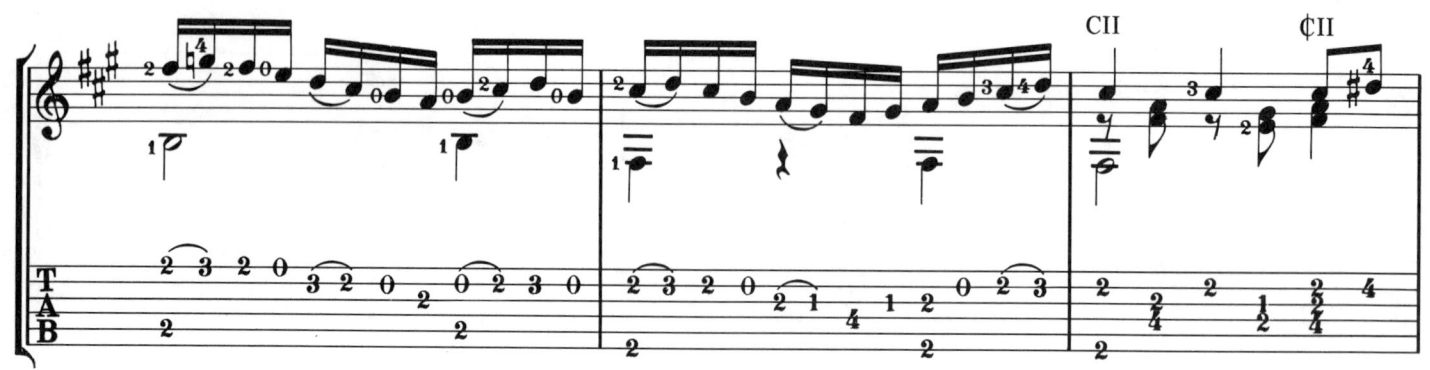

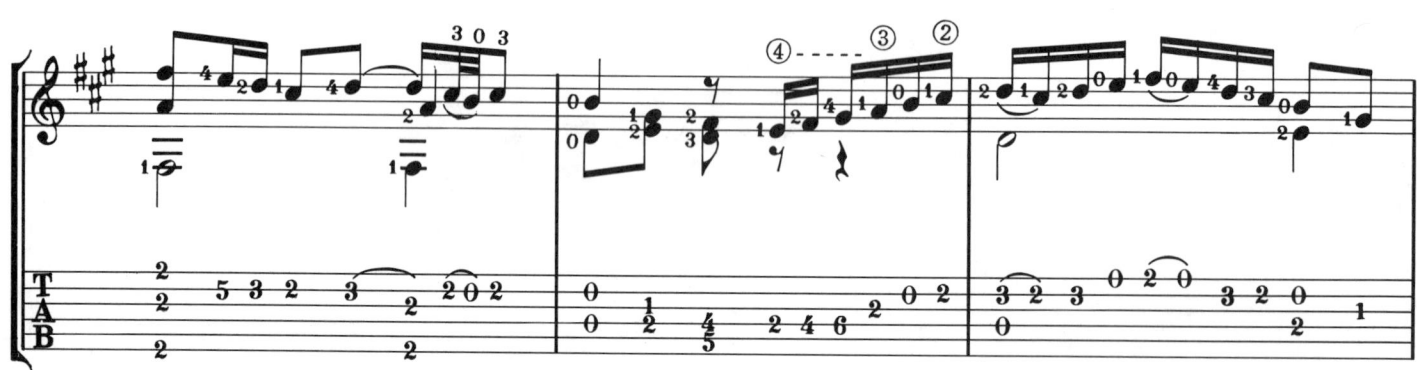
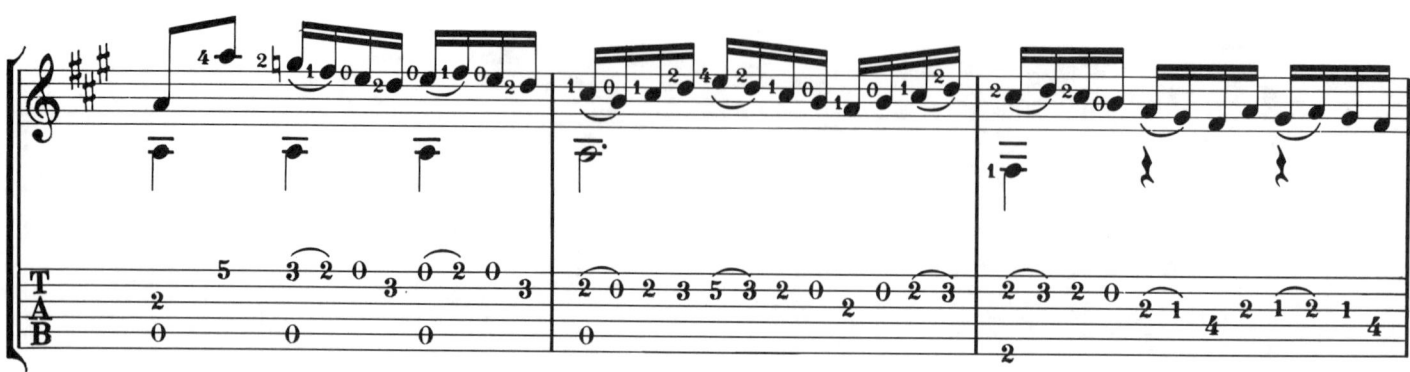

ALLEMANDE

Arr. Ben Bolt

J. S. BACH

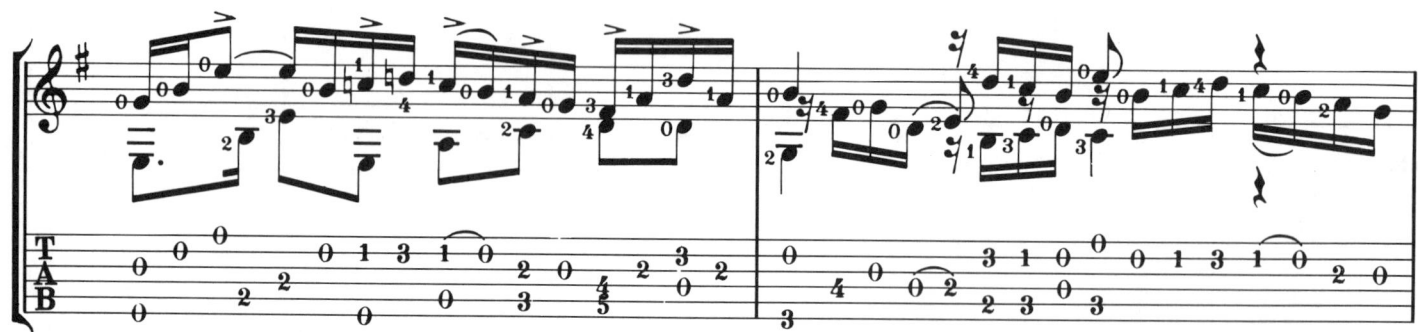

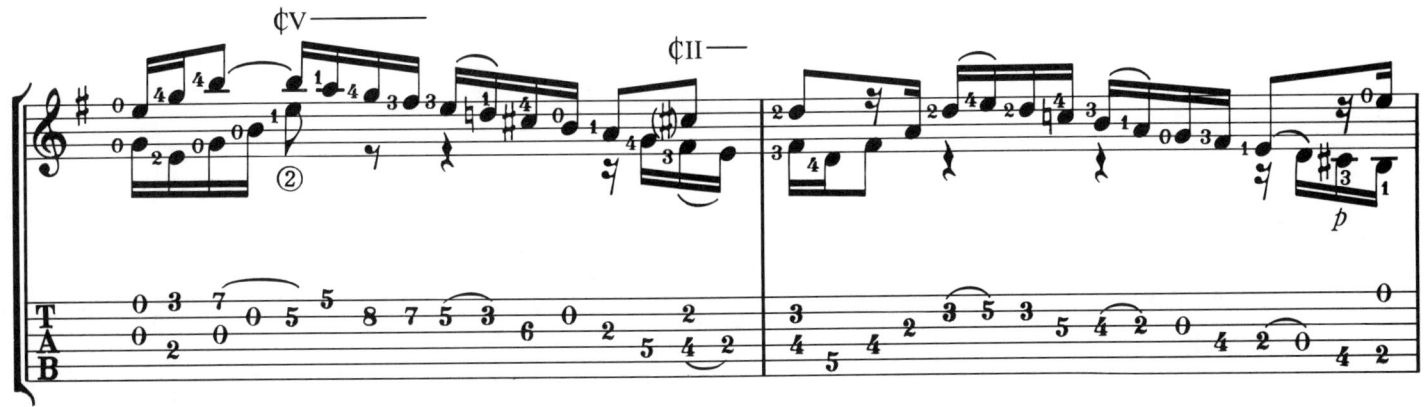

12

CANARIOS

Arr. Ben Bolt

Gaspar Sanz

This Arrangement © 1991 Cherry Lane Music Company, Inc.
International Copyright Secured All Rights Reserved

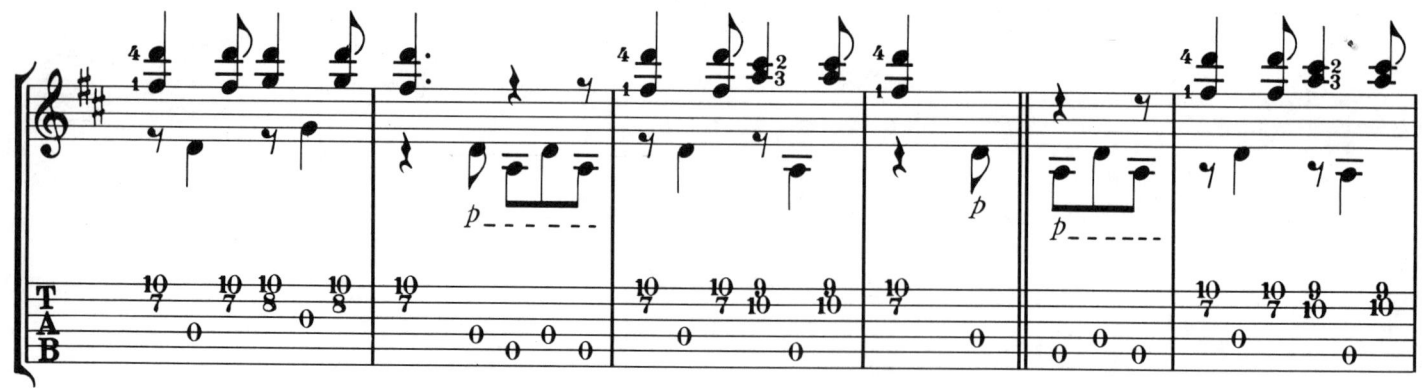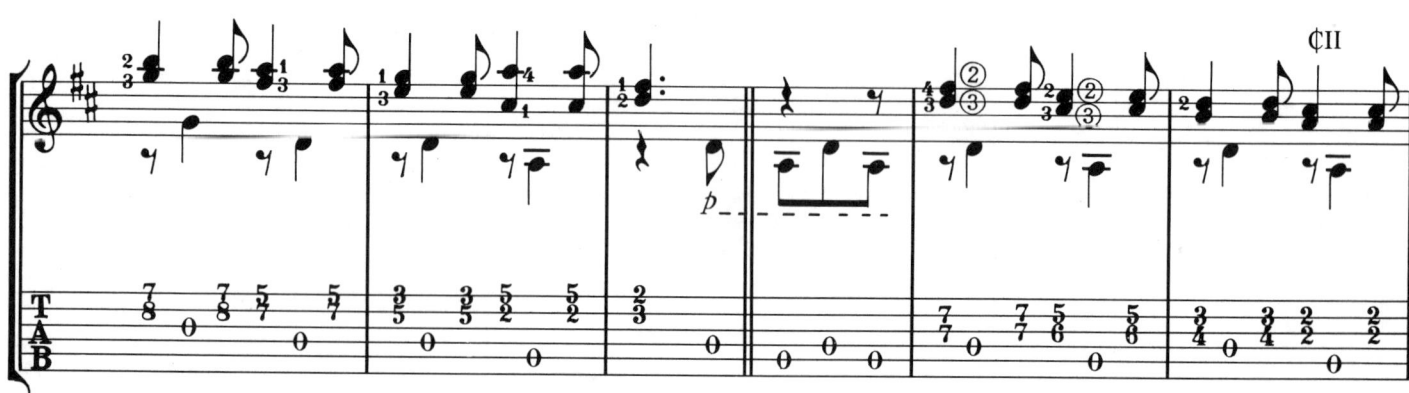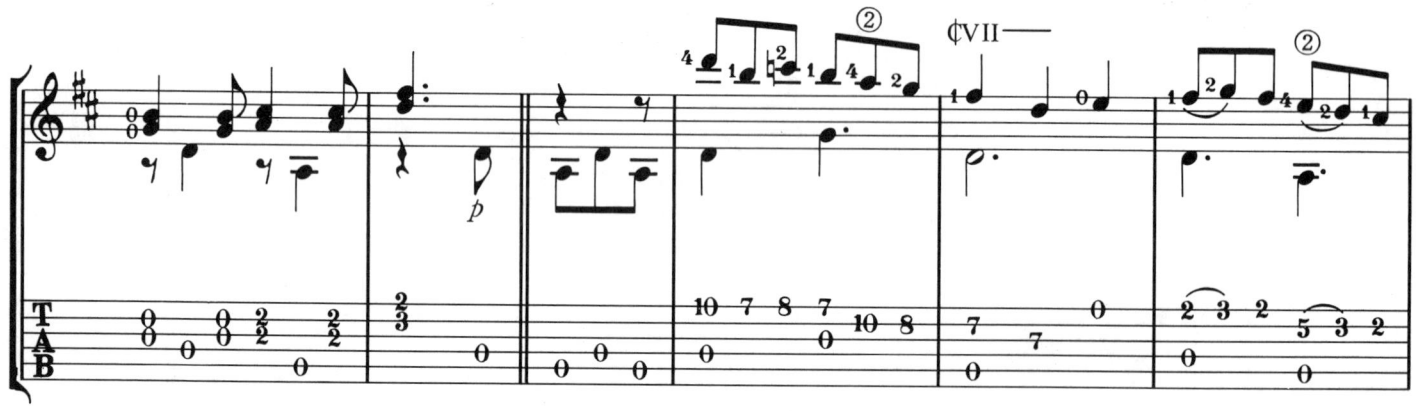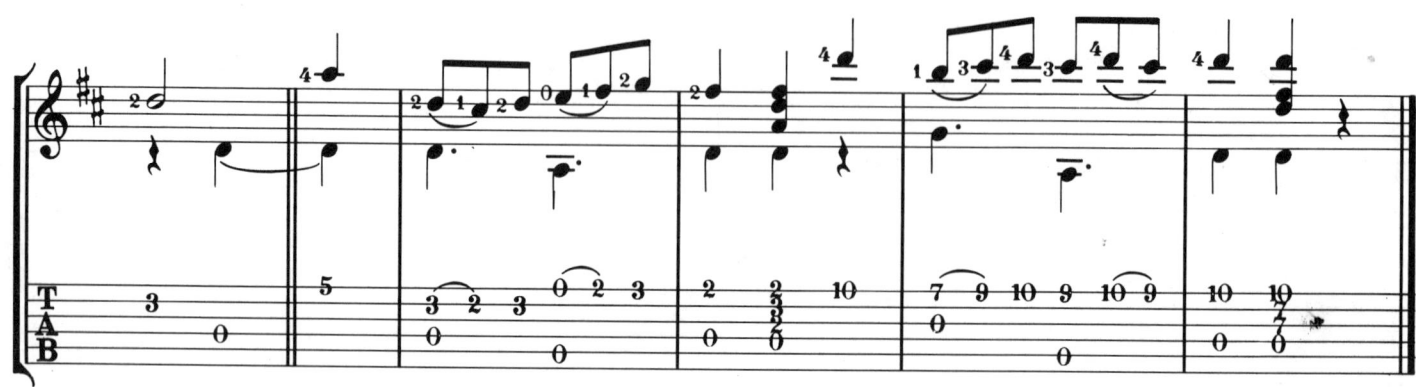